Workbook

for Key Stage 3

powered by **MyMaths**.co.uk

OXFORD
UNIVERSITY PRESS

Great Clarendon Street, Oxford, OX2 6DP, United Kingdom

Oxford University Press is a department of the University of Oxford.
It furthers the University's objective of excellence in research,
scholarship, and education by publishing worldwide. Oxford is a
registered trade mark of Oxford University Press in the UK and in
certain other countries

British Library Cataloguing in Publication Data
Data available

978-0-19-830473-9

10 9 8 7 6 5 4

Paper used in the production of this book is a natural, recyclable
product made from wood grown in sustainable forests.
The manufacturing process conforms to the environmental
regulations of the country of origin.

Printed in Great Britain by Ashford Colour Press Ltd

To multiply a number by 10, you move each digit 1 place to the left.

H	T	U	•	$\frac{1}{10}$
	2	9	•	
2	9	0	•	0

29 x 10 = 290

To divide a number by 10, you move each digit 1 place to the right.

H	T	U	•	$\frac{1}{10}$
	3	1	•	
		3	•	1

31 ÷ 10 = 3.1

1 Use these diagrams to work out these calculations.

a

H	T	U	•	$\frac{1}{10}$
	7	9	•	
7	9	0	•	

79 x 10 = __290__

b

H	T	U	•	$\frac{1}{10}$
	2	•	8	
2	8	•		

2.8 x 10 = __28__

c

H	T	U	•	$\frac{1}{10}$
1	0	3	•	
1	0	•	3	

103 ÷ 10 = __10.3__

2 Write the missing inputs and outputs for these machines.

a 29 ⟶ [x 10] ⟹ __290__

b __13__ ⟶ [x 10] ⟹ 130

c 84 ⟶ [÷10] ⟹ __8.4__

d 5.6 ⟶ [x 10] ⟹ __56__

e __62__ ⟶ [÷10] ⟹ 6.2

3 This shape is a trapezium.
It is not drawn to size.

a What is the perimeter of the trapezium?

Perimeter = __44__ cm

Imagine that the trapezium has been enlarged to make each side 10 times longer.

b Write the new measurements on this diagram.

c Calculate the new perimeter.

Perimeter = __98__ cm

```
 24
 33
 24
 17
____
 98
```

15
11
18

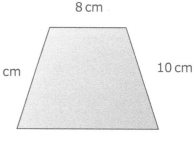

8 cm

11 cm   10 cm

15 cm

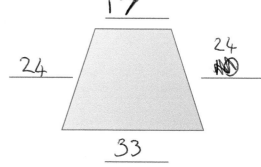

17

24   24

33

I can do this page!

1 Write down the lengths of these lines to the nearest centimetre.

a 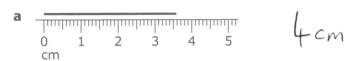   4 cm

b 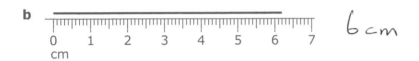   6 cm

c 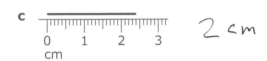   2 cm

d 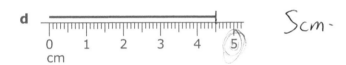   5 cm

2 Measure these lines.
  Write the length to the nearest whole centimetre.

a _____   11 cm

b _____   7 cm

c _____   6 cm

3 a Draw the shortest line along this ruler that could be rounded up to 4 cm.

b Draw the longest line along this ruler that could be rounded down to 5 cm.

5.4

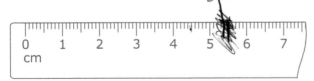

MyMaths.co.uk

Q 1003, 1004   SEARCH

1 a There are 6 different ways to group 12 students.
Write them on the diagram.
The first 2 are done for you.

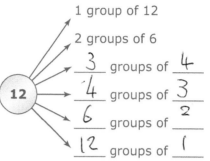

12

1 group of 12
2 groups of 6
_3_ groups of _4_
_4_ groups of _3_
_6_ groups of _2_
_12_ groups of _1_

b There are 8 different ways to group 24 students.
Write them on the diagram.

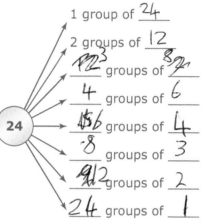

24

1 group of _24_
2 groups of _12_
_3_ groups of _8_
_4_ groups of _6_
_6_ groups of _4_
_8_ groups of _3_
_12_ groups of _2_
_24_ groups of _1_

2 a List the first 7 multiples of 3: _3_, _6_, _9_, _12_, (_15_), _18_, _21_

b List the first 7 multiples of 5: _5_, _10_, (_15_) _20_, _25_, _30_, _35_

c Circle the common multiples of 3 and 5 in your lists.

3 a List the first 8 multiples of 4: _4_, _8_, (_12_) _16_, _20_, (_24_), _28_, _32_

b List the first 8 multiples of 3: _3_, (_6_) _9_, (_12_), _15_, _18_, _21_, (_24_)

c Circle the common multiples of 4 and 3 in your lists.

d What is the lowest common multiple of 3 and 4? _12_

I can do this page!

1

A prime number has only two factors.

▶ 3 is a prime number because it has only two factors: 1 and 3.

▶ 3 can only be made by multiplying 3 × 1 or 1 × 3.

a Shade all the other prime numbers on this table.

b How many times does each prime number appear in the table?

_____

×	1	2	3	4	5	6	7	8
1	1	2	3	4	5	6	7	8
2	2	4	6	8	10	12	14	16
3	3	6	9	12	15	18	21	24
4	4	8	12	16	20	24	28	32
5	5	10	15	20	25	30	35	40
6	6	12	18	24	30	36	42	48
7	7	14	21	28	35	42	49	56
8	8	16	24	32	40	48	56	64

2 Complete these diagrams to find the prime factors of these numbers.
Shade the circles with prime numbers.
The first one has been done for you.

You will need to add more circles.

a
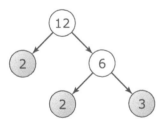

b
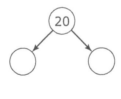

c
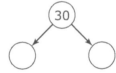

d
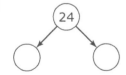

e
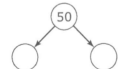

f
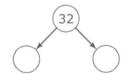

MyMaths.co.uk

1032, 1034, 1044 | SEARCH

I can do
this page!

1   Write the missing decimal numbers in the empty boxes on these
    number lines.

a

b

c

d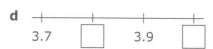

2   Estimate the positions of these numbers on this number line.
    Use arrows to point to your estimates.

a   2.1

b   4.5

c   3.8

d   4.25

3   Fill in these numbers on this place value table.

10.2

3.5

15.3

9.0

0.7

T	U	•	$\frac{1}{10}$
		•	
		•	
		•	
		•	
		•	
		•	

Use your table to write the numbers in order, smallest first.

Smallest   Greatest

_____   _____   _____   _____   _____

1   The diagram shows 8 shapes drawn on a grid.

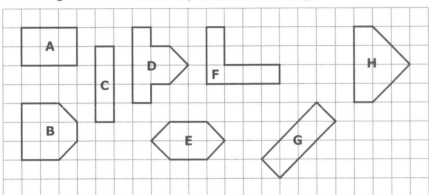

a   What are their areas?

A_____units² B_____units² C_____units² D_____units²

E_____units² F_____units² G_____units² H_____units²

b   Which 4 shapes have the same area?

Shape_____   Shape_____   Shape_____   Shape_____

2   a   What is the area of this shape?

Area = _____ cm²

b   What is the perimeter of the shape?

Perimeter = _____ cm

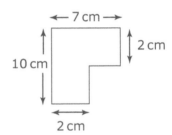

MyMaths.co.uk

Q 1084   SEARCH

1 Work out the area of each rectangle.
The drawings are not to size.

a
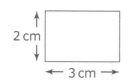
2 cm
3 cm

Area = _____ cm²

b

2 cm
10 cm

Area = _____ cm²

c
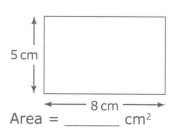
5 cm
8 cm

Area = _____ cm²

2 Work out the area of each rectangle and each shaded triangle.

a
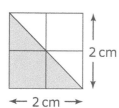
2 cm
2 cm

Area of rectangle = _____ cm²

Area of triangle = _____ cm²

b
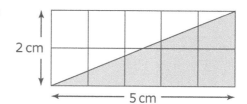
2 cm
5 cm

Area of rectangle = _____ cm²

Area of triangle = _____ cm²

c
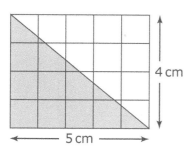
4 cm
5 cm

Area of rectangle = _____ cm²

Area of triangle = _____ cm²

d
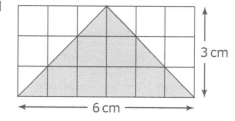
3 cm
6 cm

Area of rectangle = _____ cm²

Area of triangle = _____ cm²

3 What is the area of this triangle?
Show your working out.

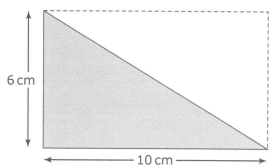
6 cm
10 cm

Area of triangle = _____ cm²

1   Complete these calculations.

    a 3 × (2 + 5) = _____   **b** 6 × (7 + 4) = _____

    c 7 × (3 + 8) = _____   **d** 10 × (8 ÷ 4) = _____

    e 4 × (12 − 4) = _____   **f** 20 × (13 − 8) = _____

2   Add brackets to these calculations to make the answer correct.

    a 2 × 7 − 1   = 13   **b** 3 × 5 + 6 = 21

    c 7 × 3 − 2   = 7   **d** 8 + 4 ÷ 3 = 4

    e 10 ÷ 2 − 3 = 2   **f** 10 ÷ 2 − 1 = 10

    g 20 − 4 ÷ 4 = 4   **h** 20 ÷ 4 − 2 = 10

    i 60 + 15 ÷ 5 = 15

3   Write numbers in the brackets to make the answer correct.

    a 4 × (___ − ___) = 20   **b** 5 × (___ + ___) = 40

    c 3 × (___ ÷ ___) = 12   **d** 8 × (___ − ___) = 24

    e 9 × (___ − ___) = 27   **f** 6 × (___ − ___) = −6

4   The perimeter of this rectangle is 24 cm.

    Perimeter = 2 × (length + width)

    Find some different measurements for the length and width of the rectangle.

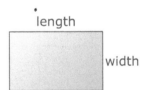

length

width

    a length _____ cm and width _____ cm

    b length _____ cm and width _____ cm

    c length _____ cm and width _____ cm

MyMaths.co.uk

Q 1247   SEARCH

3c Formulae

 I can do this page!

1   Here are 3 values:

$x = 10$, $y = 3$ and $z = 5$

Substitute these values into the expressions in this magic square.

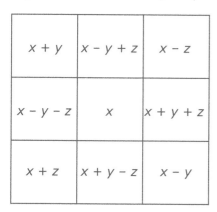

$x + y$	$x - y + z$	$x - z$
$x - y - z$	x	$x + y + z$
$x + z$	$x + y - z$	$x - y$

Write your answers in this magic square. 3 have been done for you.

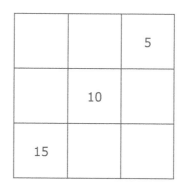

		5
	10	
15		

2   You can calculate the perimeter of a rectangle using this formula:

Perimeter = $2 \times (l + w)$

where

l = length of rectangle
w = width of rectangle.

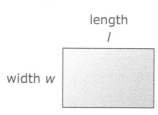

length
l

width w

Substitute the values for the length and width into the formula to calculate these perimeters.

a $l = 7\,cm$, $w = 3\,cm$

Perimeter: _____ cm

b $l = 15\,cm$, $w = 9\,cm$

Perimeter: _____ cm

c $l = 8\,mm$, $w = 2\,mm$

Perimeter: _____ mm

d $l = 25\,m$, $w = 24\,m$

Perimeter: _____ m

3   Here are some values:

$l = 8$, $d = 5$, $w = 2$

Substitute these values to work out the perimeter of this octagon.

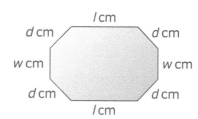

l cm
d cm d cm
w cm w cm
d cm d cm
l cm

Perimeter: _____ cm

 MyMaths.co.uk   Q 1158, 1187 SEARCH

1 Inside the bag there are *n* sweets.
Outside the bag there are 4 sweets.
Altogether there are *n* + 4 sweets.

Write an expression to say how many
sweets there are in each picture.

a

_____ sweets

b

_____ sweets

c

_____ sweets

2 There are *m* matches in a box.
This picture shows *m* + 5 matches.
You could show this in a diagram like this:

|||| ☐

Draw diagrams to show:

a *m* + 2 matches   **b** *m* matches   **c** 2*m* + 3 matches

3 **a** Write the shortest expression you can
for the perimeter of this triangle.

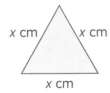

x cm   *x* cm

x cm

Perimeter = _____ cm

b Label this triangle so that
it has perimeter 2*x* + *y* cm.

Bikes are ingeniously simple structures which are very efficient at getting us around quickly and cheaply. This case study shows how bikes have developed over the years into the sophisticated machines they are today.

Task 1

The pedals of a penny-farthing bicycle were fixed directly to the front wheel so the wheel turned once for every turn of the pedals. The larger the wheel, the further the bike travelled for each turn.

Task 2

If you remember riding a tricycle like this, you will know that you had to pedal quite quickly even at low speeds!

This penny-farthing has a wheel diameter of 1 m.

a How far would the bike travel for one turn of the pedals?
   Remember: $C = \pi d$
   Use $\pi \approx 3$

b How far would the bike travel for two turns of the pedals?

c Ten turns?

d 50 turns?

e How many turns of the pedals would be needed to travel 3 km?

a With a 30 cm diameter front wheel, how many turns of the pedals would be needed to travel 900 m?

b Why does a child have to pedal quickly on this type of tricycle?

1 **a** Shade $\frac{1}{5}$ of this grid.

   b Use your drawing to complete these equivalent fractions.

$$\frac{}{15} = \frac{1}{5}$$

   c Shade $\frac{1}{3}$ of this grid.

   d Use your drawing to complete these equivalent fractions.

$$\frac{}{15} = \frac{1}{3}$$

   e Use your grids to answer these questions.

   i $\frac{1}{3} + \frac{1}{5} = \frac{}{15}$ **ii** $\frac{1}{3} - \frac{1}{5} = \frac{}{15}$

2 **a** Shade $\frac{1}{5}$ of this grid.   **b** Shade $\frac{1}{4}$ of this grid.

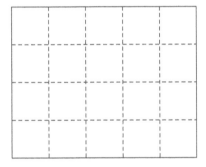   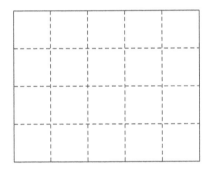

   c Use your grids to answer these questions.

   i $\frac{1}{4} + \frac{1}{5} = \frac{}{20}$ **ii** $\frac{1}{4} - \frac{1}{5} = \frac{}{20}$

⊞ **MyMaths**.co.uk   Q 1017   **SEARCH**

1 **a** Circle $\frac{1}{4}$ of these tiles.

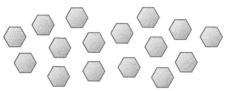

> Remember: to find $\frac{1}{4}$, you divide by 4.

  b Complete this statement:

  $\frac{1}{4}$ of 16 = _____

2 **a** Here are 12 tiles. Shade $\frac{1}{3}$ of them.

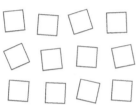

  b What is $\frac{1}{3}$ of 12? _____

  c What is $\frac{2}{3}$ of 12? _____

3 These hexagon tiles are $\frac{2}{5}$ of a larger pattern.

  How many tiles are there in the larger pattern?

  Answer: _____ tiles

4 One quarter $\left(\frac{1}{4}\right)$ of the wall has been tiled.

  How many tiles will be needed for the whole wall?

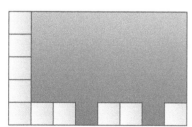

  Answer: _____ tiles

1 This box has been divided into 10 equal parts.

10%	10%	10%	10%	10%
10%	10%	10%	10%	10%

Each of the 10 parts is 10%.

a So far 14 dots have been shared.
   Share out dots equally until you have shared 50 in total.
   The number of dots in each box is 10% of 50.

b What is 10% of 50? _____

c What is 20% of 50? _____

d What is 70% of 50? _____

2 Use this box to work out 70% of 70.

10%	10%	10%	10%	10%
10%	10%	10%	10%	10%

Hint: First work out
10% of 70. You could
share out 70 dots.

70% of 70 = _____

3 a Calculate 10% of 90. 10% of 90 = _____

   b Use your answer to calculate 40% of 90.

      40% of 90 = _____

MyMaths.co.uk

Q 1030, 1031 SEARCH

1   Fill in the missing information about each triangle.

   a   Equilateral triangle

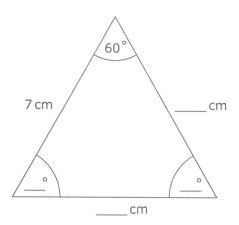

   b   Isosceles triangle

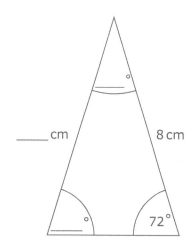

2   **a**   Measure the 3 angles of this triangle.
        Write them on the diagram.

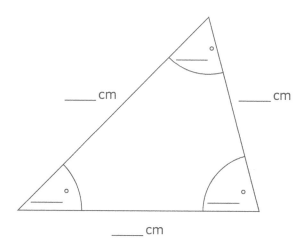

   b   Add the 3 angles together.

        _____° + _____° + _____° = _____°

   c   Measure the 3 sides of this triangle.
        Write the lengths on the diagram.

   d   What type of triangle is this? _____

For each question:

a Join the dots to make a quadrilateral.

Use a ruler!

b Name the shape.

c Fill in the missing parts of the description.

---

1 Name _____

   1   2

5

                     ____ equal angles

                     4 equal sides

                     2 sets parallel sides

4   3

2 Name _____

   1   2 2 pairs of equal angles

5

                    4 equal sides

                   ____ sets of parallel sides

4   3

---

3 Name _____

2   3

   1
    5   4

2 pairs of equal angles

____ sets of equal sides

2 sets of parallel sides

4 Name _____

2   3 ____ equal angles

                  2 sets of equal sides

1   2 sets of parallel
5   4 sides

---

5 Name _____

4   5
        1

Usually has:

   no equal angles

   no equal sides

Always has:

3   2 ____ set of parallel sides

6 Name _____

  1   2 ____ sets of equal angles

5

                  1 set of equal sides

4   3 1 set of parallel sides

---

7 Name _____

   3   1 pair of equal angles

2   4 2 sets of equal sides

                ____ parallel sides

    1 5

8 Name _____

     2 1 pair of equal angles

                ____ sets of equal sides

1   4   3
5   No parallel sides

MyMaths.co.uk

Q 1141   **SEARCH**

1 a Measure the 4 angles of this quadrilateral.

Write the angles on the diagram.

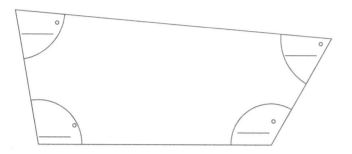

b Add the 4 angles together.

_____° + _____° + _____° + _____° = _____°

c Complete this statement:

▶ The sum of the angles in a quadrilateral is _____°.

2 Write in the missing angles in these quadrilaterals.

a

b

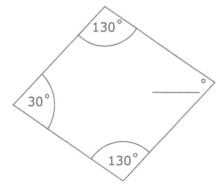

130°

30°

130°

c

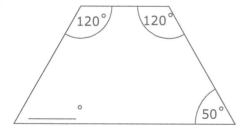

120°   120°

50°

d

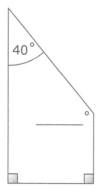

40°

I can do this page! ✓

1 a Complete the table of values for this equation: $y = x - 4$

x	0	1	2	3	4	5
−4	−4	−4	−4	−4	−4	−4
y		−3				

b Plot the x- and y-coordinates onto this grid.

c Join your points to make a straight line.

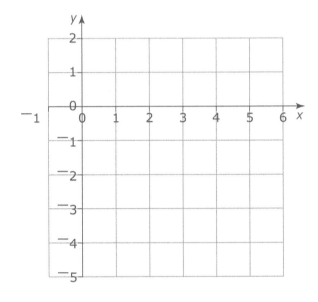

2 a Complete the table of values for this equation: $y = x + 2$

x	−1	0	1	2	3	4	5
+2	+2	+2	+2				
y							

b Number the axes.

c Plot the x- and y-coordinates on this grid.

d Join your points to make a straight line.

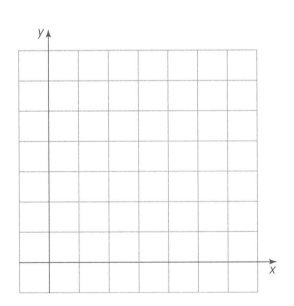

MyMaths.co.uk

Q 1168 | SEARCH

1 Calculate the outputs from these function machines

  a 3 ⟶ ×4 ⟹ − 2 ⟹ _____

  b 4 ⟶ ×3 ⟹ + 1 ⟹ _____

  c 10 ⟶ ×2 ⟹ + 3 ⟹ _____

  d 12 ⟶ ÷ 4 ⟹ + 2 ⟹ _____

2 For the equation $y = 2x + 3$:

  a Use this machine to calculate the values in the table.

  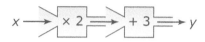

  x ⟶ ×2 ⟹ + 3 ⟹ y

x	0	1	2	3	4	5
y						

  b Write the coordinate pairs:

  (0, ____)   (1, ____)   (____, ____)

  (____, ____) (____, ____) (____, ____)

  c Plot the x- and y-coordinates onto this grid.

  d Join your points to make a straight line.

  e Label your line: $y = 2x + 3$.

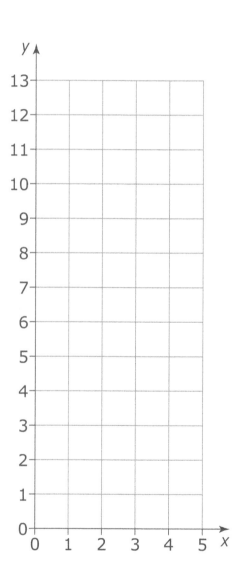

1 Draw graphs of these journeys on the axes.

a Jan walks 5 km in 2 hours

b Ali cycles 4 km in $1\frac{1}{2}$ hours

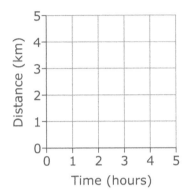

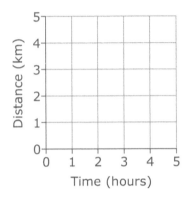

2

The line on the graph shows a journey of 6 km takes 2 hours, or 3 km per hour.
The speed shown by the graph line is 3 km/h.

On this grid draw lines to show journeys of these speeds.

a 6 km/h

b 2 km/h

c 3.5 km/h

d 1.5 km/h

e 0.5 km/h

Draw your lines to the edge of the grid.
Label your lines.
The first line has been drawn for you.

f Which line shows a journey of 3 km in 2 hours?

Line _____

g If your speed is 3.5 km/h, how far will you travel in 3 hours? _____ km

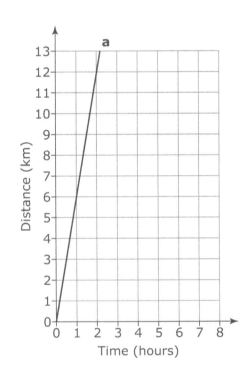

MyMaths.co.uk

Q 1184   SEARCH

 I can do this page!

1 Each week the number of merits earned by Year 9 students are counted.
   The frequency table shows this week's results.
   Put this data onto the bar chart.

Class	9A	9B	9C	9D	9E
Number of merits	33	25	45	35	40

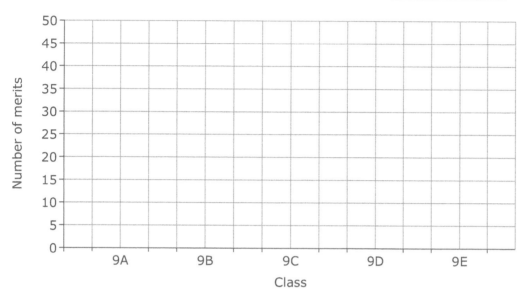

2 The frequency table shows the average maximum temperature
   for each month in the year. Put this data onto the line graph.

Month	Jan	Feb	Mar	Apr	May	Jun	Jul	Aug	Sep	Oct	Nov	Dec
Temp. °C	11°	13°	15°	17°	18°	20°	22°	24°	23°	19°	16°	12°

Katie and Jess are going to make bracelets and necklaces to sell on an online auction site. They need to ensure that they keep their costs down, to help them run a profitable business.

Katie and Jess have found out the cost of materials from two suppliers.

Each supplier quotes prices for two types of bead—long ones or round ones.

They also quote prices for waxed cord or leather thread.

length
16mm beads

length
8mm beads

  NATURAL BEAD COMPANY

16mm beads	8mm beads
£10.00 per 250	£5.00 per 250

Leather thread	Waxed cord
£12.00 per 50m	£2.00 per 50m

Task 1

a Katie and Jess want 500 beads of each size. Which supplier should they use? Show your workings out.

b They also want 50m of leather thread, as well as 50m of waxed cord. Again, decide which supplier they should use, showing clearly your workings out.

(2) BEAD-E-IZE

16mm beads	8mm beads	Waxed cord
£18.00 per 500	£9.00 per 500	

Leather thread	Waxed cord	Leather thread
£2.00 per 10m	£3.00 per 25m	

Task 2

Katie and Jess want their bracelets to be 16cm long, with an adjustable tie. Only ¾ of this length can be used for beads.

a How many long beads would fit on a bracelet?

b How many round beads would fit on a bracelet?

Task 3

Katie and Jess want their necklaces to be 30cm long. Only ²/₃ of this length can be used for beads.

a How many long beads would fit on a necklace?

b How many round beads would fit on a necklace?

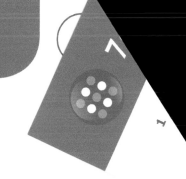

1 Fill in the missing numbers as quickly as you can.

a 6 × ____ = 12

b 4 × ____ = 24

c ____ × 3 = 27

d 7 × ____ = 21

e 5 × ____ = 40

f 3 × ____ = 24

g ____ × 8 = 64

h 5 × ____ = 35

2 Fill in the missing numbers as quickly as you can.

a 36 ÷ 6 = ____

b 55 ÷ 5 = ____

c 48 ÷ 6 = ____

d 28 ÷ 4 = ____

e 24 ÷ 3 = ____

f 35 ÷ 7 = ____

g 72 ÷ 8 = ____

h 54 ÷ 9 = ____

Use tables to multiply these decimal numbers by 10.
The first one has been done for you.

a
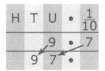

$9.7 \times 10 = 97$ or 97.0

b
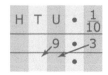

$9.3 \times 10 = \underline{\hspace{1cm}}$

c
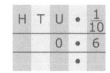

$0.6 \times 10 = \underline{\hspace{1cm}}$

d
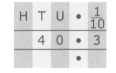

$28.1 \times 10 = \underline{\hspace{1cm}}$

e

$40.3 \times 10 = \underline{\hspace{1cm}}$

f
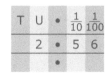

$2.56 \times 10 = \underline{\hspace{1cm}}$

2 Calculate the outputs for these inputs in your head,
and write the answers.

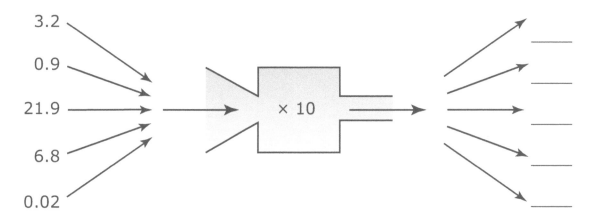

3.2

0.9

21.9

6.8

0.02

× 10

3 Calculate the outputs for the inputs in these 2-stage machines.

a 1.2 → × 10 → 12 → × 2 → ____

b 3.5 → × 10 → ____ → × 3 → ____

c 5.6 → × 10 → ____ → × 3 → ____

d 12.1 → × 10 → ____ → × 5 → ____

1   James used a calculator to work out these answers.
    Write the calculator display for each one.
    The first one has been done for you.

a £2.90

b £13.70

c £12.08

d £5.09

e 25p

f 3p

2 **a** Use the clues in the table to calculate the missing distances.
         Write the distances onto the diagram.

Distance	Clue
A to B	From A to B to C is 150.3 km. From B to C is 75.9 km.
A to C (direct)	The direct distance from A to C is twice the distance from A to B.
C to D	The distance from C to D is a quarter of the distance from C to E.
D to E	The distance from D to E is 3 and a half times the distance from C to D.

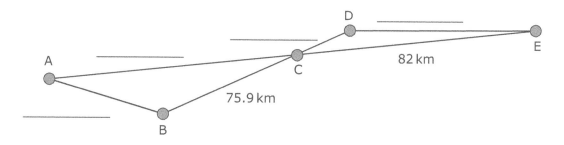

   b Which is the shortest distance: A to E (direct) or B to D (direct)?
          _____ to _____

   Explain how you calculated your answer.

   _____

   _____

8c Frequency tables

I can do this page!

1 Look around the room you are in.

  a Use tallies to record the colour of objects in the room in this data collection sheet.
     You are looking for blue, red, yellow and green objects.
     Stop after 5 minutes.

Colour of object	Tally	Frequency
Blue		
Red		
Yellow		
Green		

  b Count the tallies and write in the frequency for each colour.

  c What is the most common colour? _____

2 Samantha asks 25 people to name their favourite fruit.
  Here are their replies:

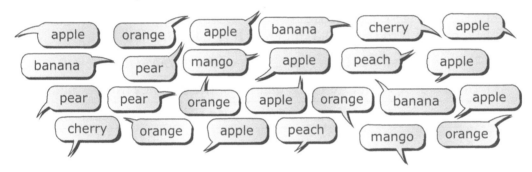

  a Complete this data collection sheet for this information.

Fruit	Tally	Frequency

  b Which is the most popular fruit? _____

  c Which are the least popular fruit? _____

MyMaths.co.uk   Q 1193   SEARCH

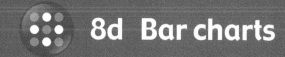

5 classes are involved in a sports quiz.
Here are their scores:

9D = 14 points

9G = 22 points

9K = 13 points

9W = 25 points

9Y = 19 points

Put this data onto a chart.
Make sure your chart has a title and
the axes are labelled. Colour it in.

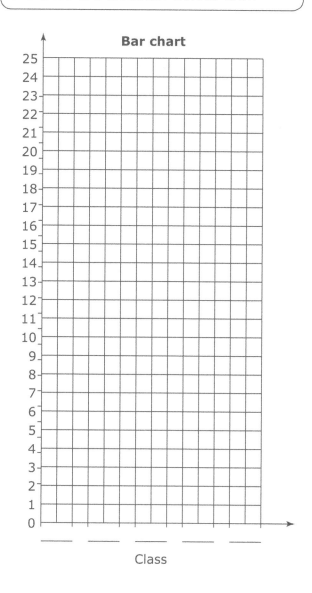

Bar chart

Class

 I can do this page!

▶ The mode is the most common value.
▶ The median is the middle value when the data are in order.
▶ The mean is the total divided by the number of values.

1 a What is the mode of this data?

2, 5, 3, 6, 5, 2, 5, 1, 1, 5   Mode: _____5_____

b What is the mode of this data?

2, 2, 3, 7, 5, 7, 1, 4, 3, 8, 7, 2   Mode: ___7___ and ___2___

2 a What is the median of this data?   1,2,8,12,14,15,19

14, 2, 15, 8, 14, 12, 8, 19, 1

Write the data in order, smallest to largest, to help you.

Data in order: _1,2,8,8_____   Median: _14_

b What is the median of this data?

13, 6, 22, 6, 13, 9, 8, 17

Data in order: _6,6,8,9,13,13,17,22____   Median: ___9___

3 Calculate the mean of each set of data.

a 6, 2, 9, 12, 1   Mean: ___6___

b 10, 3, 7, 5, 8, 6   39   Mean: ~~38~~ 6.3

4 A group of students are asked how many 'take-away' meals they eat each month. Here are the results.

3, 2, 6, 2, 4, 2, 6, 5, 2, 3

a What is the mode of this data?   Mode: ___2___

b What is the median of this data?   Median: ~~3~~2.5

c What is the mean of this data?   Mean: 3.5

35   2, 2, 2, 2, 3, 3, 4, 5, 6

6   12   18   24   30   36

1 A group of college students sit a test.

The results are shown on this stem-and-leaf diagram.

10	1	2	2	6		
20	0	4	5	8	8	9
30	3	8	9			
40	0	0	0	6	8	
50	8	9	9			

Key:

40 | 5
represents 45

a How many students scored 20 marks? _____students

b How many students scored 52 marks? _____students

c What is the **range** of marks? _____marks

d What is the **mode** of the data? _____marks

e The 'pass mark' was 25.
How many students failed? _____students

2 These are the numbers of items purchased by 20 customers in a supermarket.

2, 5, 5, 11, 12, 12, 16, 18, 21, 22, 22,
24, 25, 27, 28, 30, 35, 36, 36, 43

a Put this data onto the stem-and-leaf diagram.

0	
10	
20	
30	
40	

Key:

10 | 2
represents 12

b What is the **range** of the number of items purchased? _____items

c What are the **modes** of the data? _____items

8i Frequency diagrams

I can do
this page!

1   Here is a record of the exam marks of 70 Year 9 students.

3	9	13	13	14	18	19	22	23	25
29	32	35	37	43	45	49	50	53	54
54	56	57	59	60	61	63	67	68	70
71	71	72	73	75	76	76	78	79	80
81	83	83	83	85	87	88	88	90	91
92	93	95	95	96	97	97	98	99	100
100	103	105	106	109	111	111	112	115	118

What is the range of this data? _____

2   Tally the marks onto this frequency table.
The size of each interval is 20.

Number of marks	Tally	Frequency
0–19		
20–39		
40–59		
60–79		
80–99		
100–119		

3   Complete this bar chart using your frequency table.

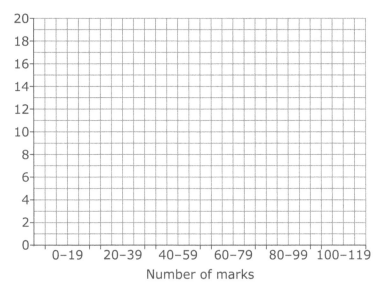

Number of marks

MyMaths.co.uk   1196   SEARCH

Here are 6 regular polygons.

Draw all the lines of symmetry on each polygon.

a

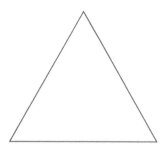

Equilateral triangle

b

Square

c

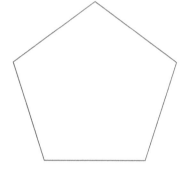

Pentagon

d

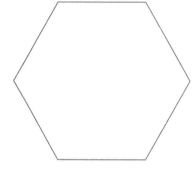

Hexagon

e

Heptagon

f

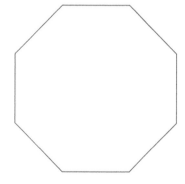

Octagon

1 a Draw the reflection of the shape in the mirror line.

  b Label the reflection A', B', C', D' and E'.

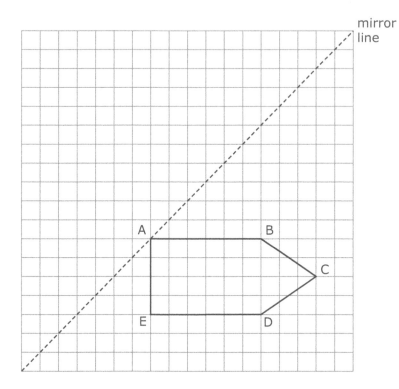

Remember:

The object and the image are the same distance from the mirror line.

If you draw a line from the object to the image it is perpendicular to the mirror line.

MyMaths.co.uk

Q 1113 SEARCH

1 Translate the shape following each of these instructions.
Start from the original shape each time.

   a 3 down then 4 left.
   4 up.

   Label your shape A.

   b 6 left then 1 up.
   5 down.

   Label your shape B.

   c 1 right then 5 down.
   2 left then 1 up.

   Label your shape C.

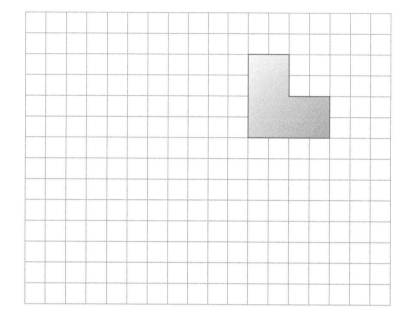

2 Match each vector to the translation it describes.

   The first one has been done for you.

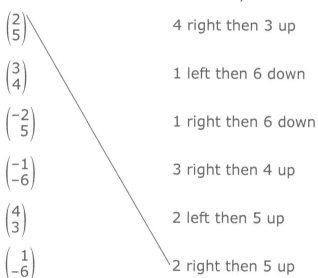

$\begin{pmatrix} 2 \\ 5 \end{pmatrix}$ 4 right then 3 up

$\begin{pmatrix} 3 \\ 4 \end{pmatrix}$ 1 left then 6 down

$\begin{pmatrix} -2 \\ 5 \end{pmatrix}$ 1 right then 6 down

$\begin{pmatrix} -1 \\ -6 \end{pmatrix}$ 3 right then 4 up

$\begin{pmatrix} 4 \\ 3 \end{pmatrix}$ 2 left then 5 up

$\begin{pmatrix} 1 \\ -6 \end{pmatrix}$ 2 right then 5 up

1   Enlarge this shape by a scale factor of 2.
The base line of the enlarged shape is drawn for you.

> Multiply all the
> lengths by the
> scale factor.

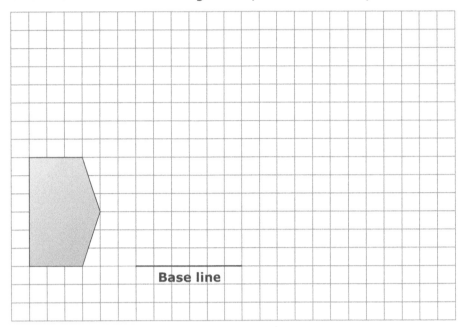

Base line

2   Enlarge this shape by a scale factor of 3.
The base line of the enlarged image is drawn for you.

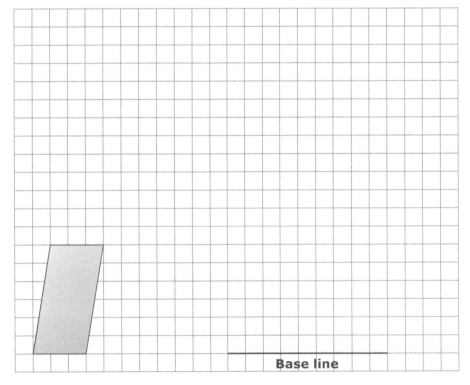

Base line

MyMaths.co.uk

🔍 1099   SEARCH

Here is the floor plan of a holiday chalet.

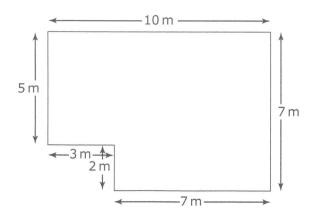

Draw the plan to scale on the grid.

Use a scale of 1 : 100 (1 cm : 1 m)

1 cm

Case study 3: Climate change

The Earth's climate has always changed due to natural causes such as change of orbit, volcanic eruptions and changes in the sun's energy, but now there is real concern that human activity is upsetting the balance by adding to 'greenhouse gases'.

Greenhouse gases

This diagram shows some of the main factors behind global warming.

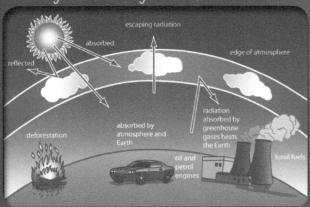

escaping radiation
absorbed
edge of atmosphere
reflected
radiation absorbed by greenhouse gases heats the Earth
deforestation
absorbed by atmosphere and Earth
oil and petrol engines
fossil fuels

[Task 1]

The pie chart shows the contribution made to the warming effect by the main greenhouse gases

- ■ carbon dioxide
- □ methane
- □ nitrous oxide
- ■ others

a Which greenhouse gas has the largest warming effect?
b Which greenhouse gas has the smallest warming effect?

[Task 2]

Burning fuel in power stations increases the carbon dioxide in the air.
You can help to reduce this by using less electricity.
a Roughly how many hours of television do you watch each day?
b So how many hours a day is your television NOT being watched?
A television uses 5 watts per hour on standby.
c How many watts of energy will be saved if the television is switched off compared with being left on standby?
d Roughly how many watts of electricity would be saved each year (365 days)?
e Roughly how many watts of electricity would be saved each year if 1000 people in a town switched off their televisions instead of leaving them on standby?

[Task 3]

Find out about your carbon footprint which measures how much you are contributing to greenhouse gases.

10a Equality and inequality

1 Calculate the weight of the grey parcel.
Write it onto the parcel.

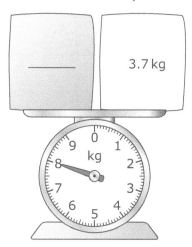

3.7 kg

2 Each of the parcels weighs the same.
Calculate the weight of each parcel.

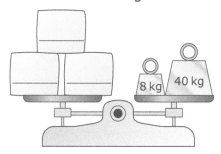

8 kg 40 kg

3 The total weight of these parcels is 8.4 kg.
The large parcel is twice the weight of the smaller ones.

a Label the parcels with their weights.

b Show the total weight on the dial.

1 Write the outputs for these operation machines.

   a 5 ⟶ ×7 ⟹ ____   **b** 100 ⟶ ÷25 ⟹ ____

2 What are the inverses of these operations?

   a ⟶ – 6 ⟹   **b** ⟶ ÷ 3 ⟹

   Inverse: _____   Inverse: _____

3 Use inverse operations to calculate the input numbers.

   a 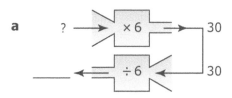   **b**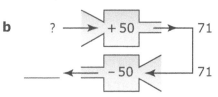

4 Write the equations shown by these diagrams.
     The first one is started for you.

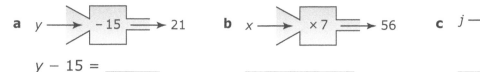

   a y ⟶ – 15 ⟹ 21   **b** x ⟶ ×7 ⟹ 56   **c** j ⟶ ÷9 ⟹ 9

   $y - 15 =$ _____   _____   _____

5 Use the machines to calculate the value of the symbol.

   a $10h = 130$ **b** $f \div 4 = 16$

   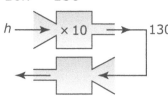   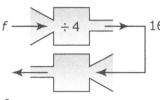

   $h =$ _____ $f =$ _____

MyMaths.co.uk   🔍 1154   **SEARCH**

10c Balancing equations 1

I can do this page!

1 Write the outputs for these machines.

a 6 ⟶ ×4 ⟹ +7 ⟹ _____

b 20 ⟶ ×5 ⟹ −13 ⟹ _____

2 This is the machine for the equation $3y + 5 = 23$.

y ⟶ ×3 ⟹ +5 ⟹ 23

Complete the machines for these equations.

a $2x − 6 = 22$

x ⟶ ☐ ⟹ ☐ ⟹ __

b $4d + 7 = 39$

d ⟶ ☐ ⟹ ☐ ⟹ __

3 Use the machines to solve these equations.

a $6x − 2 = 28$

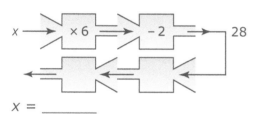

x ⟶ ×6 ⟹ −2 ⟶ 28

$x =$ _____

b $\dfrac{c}{10} + 13 = 18$

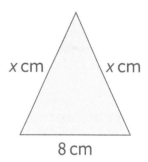

c ⟶ ÷10 ⟹ +13 ⟹ 18

$c =$ _____

4 The perimeter of this triangle is 50 cm.
The equation for its perimeter is

$2x + 8 = 50$ cm

Use this machine to solve the equation and calculate the length of side x.

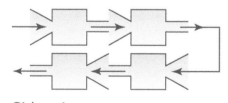

Side x is _____ cm

x cm x cm

8 cm

10d Balancing equations 2

3 cans balance with 2 boxes.

2 boxes balance with 1 bottle.

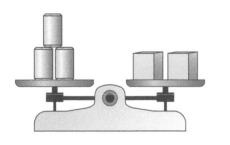
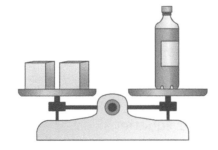

1 a Draw the boxes needed to balance with 6 cans.

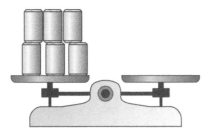

b Draw only boxes to make the scales balance.

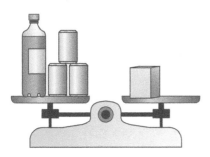

c Draw the **least** number of items to make these scales balance.

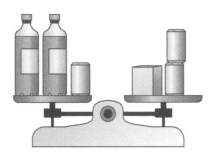

> You can use boxes, cans or bottles.

d Draw these items on the scales so that they balance.

MyMaths.co.uk

Q 1182 SEARCH

I can do this page!

1 Write an equation for each elastic band stretch. The first one is done for you.

a The elastic band is 10 cm.

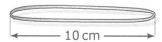
10 cm

When it is stretched it is 27 cm long.

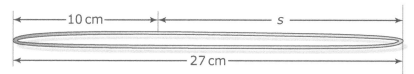
10 cm   s
27 cm

Call the 'stretch' s.

Equation: $10 + s = 27$

b The elastic band is 13 cm.

13 cm

When it is stretched it is 36 cm long.

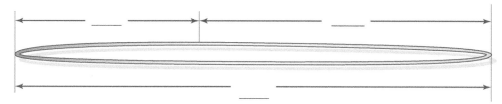

i Label the diagram.

ii Write an equation for the stretch. _____

iii Solve the equation to calculate the stretch. $s =$ _____ cm

c The elastic band is 11 cm.

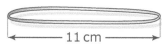
11 cm

When it is stretched it is 52 cm long.

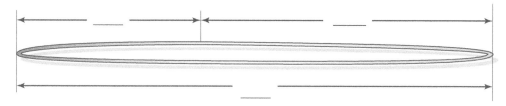

i Label the diagram.

ii Write an equation for the stretch. _____

iii Solve the equation to calculate the stretch. $s =$ _____ cm

1 a Complete this multiplication table.

b Shade all of the square numbers up to 100.

c Describe the pattern the square numbers make in the grid.

_____

_____

_____

×	2	3	4	5	6	7	8	9	10
2	4	6	8	10	12	14	16	18	20
3	6	9	12	15	18	21	24	27	30
4		12	16	20	24		32	36	40
5	10		20	25		35	40	45	50
6	12	18	24			42	48	54	60
7	14	21		35	42	49	56	63	70
8	16		32		48	56	64	72	80
9	18	27	36		54	63	72	81	90
10			40		60			90	100

2 Use this grid to find the square roots of these numbers.

a square root of 1   = _____

b square root of 16   = _____

c square root of 100   = _____

d square root of 25   = _____

e square root of 4   = _____

f square root of 49   = _____

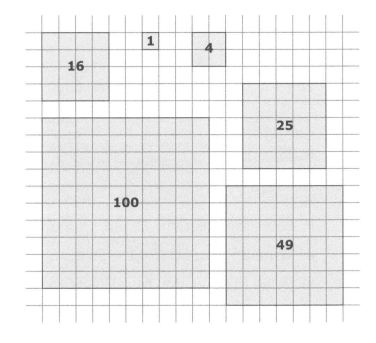

3 Complete these statements.
The first one is done for you.

a $\sqrt{25}$ = 5

b $\sqrt{}$ _____ = 4

c $\sqrt{}$ _____ = 9

d $\sqrt{}$ _____ = 1

e $\sqrt{}$ _____ = 3

f $\sqrt{}$ _____ = 6

MyMaths.co.uk   🔍 1053   SEARCH

12a Using a protractor

1   What is the missing angle in each triangle?

a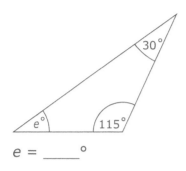

e = _____°

b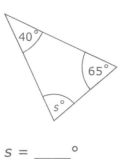

s = _____°

c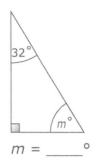

m = _____°

Hint: Do not use a protractor for question 1.

2   Measure these 2 angles with a protractor.

a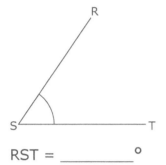

RST = _____°

b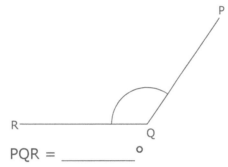

PQR = _____°

3   Construct an angle of 46° using a protractor.
    Use this base line:

    _____

4   Use a protractor, pencil and ruler to construct these triangles.
    The base line is drawn for you, and the size of each angle is given.

a   b

    _____   _____
    90°   15°   75°   25°

I can do
this page!

1 a Which line is perpendicular
     to AB? _____

   b Which line is perpendicular
     to EF? _____

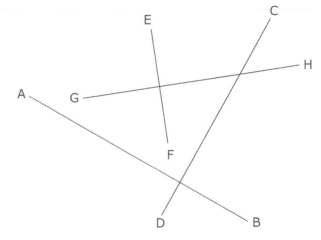

2 This is the unfinished diagram of a shed.
   Draw the sides of the shed. Use a protractor or set-square to make
   sure they are perpendicular to the ground.

roof

_____

ground

3 Mark the midpoint of this line.
   Draw a perpendicular line through the midpoint.
   Mark the right angle.

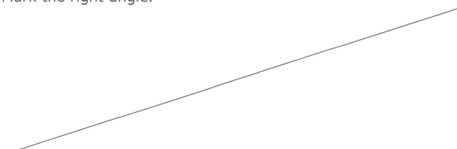

MyMaths.co.uk

Q 1089   SEARCH

Case study 4: Garden design

Sensory gardens are designed to stimulate the senses - sight, sound, smell, touch and even taste - and are thought to have a beneficial effect on people who visit them. Whilst they must be designed for all users, this case study considers their accessibility for wheelchair users.

Raised flowerbeds are easier to reach for a person in a wheelchair.

Cross section of a raised bed

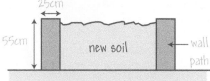

PLAN FOR A SENSORY CORNER

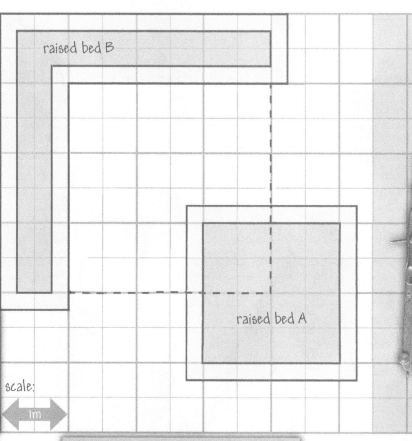

raised bed B

raised bed A

scale:

1m

Task 1

Look at the scale drawing of the garden.

Calculate the area in m² of

a) bed A   b) bed B

Task 2

Look at the cross-section diagram of a raised bed. Each bed is to be filled with soil to 5cm from the top of the wall. Calculate the volume of soil needed to fill

a) bed A   b)   bed B

Give your answers in m³

Wide paths make it easier to get around.

1 a Draw the next pattern in this dot pattern.

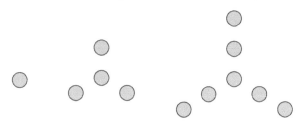

b How many dots do you add each time? _____ dots

c Complete the first 4 terms of this sequence in numbers:

1, 4, _____, _____

2 a Use dots ◯ to draw a sequence that goes up by 2 each time.
Draw 4 terms.

b Write the terms of your sequence in numbers:

_____, _____, _____, _____

3 a Use triangles △ to draw a sequence that goes down by 3 each time.
Start with 11 triangles.
Draw 4 terms.

b Write the terms of your sequence in numbers: _____, _____, _____, _____

c What are the next 2 terms in the number sequence? _____, _____

MyMaths.co.uk

Q 1173   SEARCH

13b Position-to-term rules

1 a Draw the next 2 patterns in this sequence.

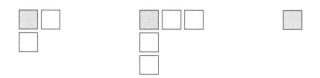

b Complete this table showing the numbers of squares in each pattern.

	1st pattern	2nd pattern	3rd pattern	4th pattern
Grey squares	1			
White squares	2			
Total	3			

c The totals from the table make a sequence. Complete the sequence for 6 patterns.

1st pattern   2nd pattern   3rd pattern   4th pattern   5th pattern   6th pattern

1 + 1 + 1   1 + 2 + 2   1 + __ + __   1 + __ + __   __ + __ + __   __ + __ + __

  = 3   = 5   = __   = __   = __   = __

d Complete this sentence and machine to describe the rule.

The rule is: multiply the pattern number by _____ and add _____

position ———→ ⟩—— ⟩ ⟩—— ⟩ ———→ term

2 a Add 2 more patterns to this sequence:

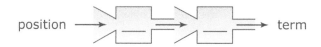

1st   2nd   3rd   4th

b Complete this table showing the numbers of dots in each pattern.

	1st pattern	2nd pattern	3rd pattern	4th pattern
Grey dots	2			
White dots	3			
Total	5			

1 Sketch these 3D shapes.

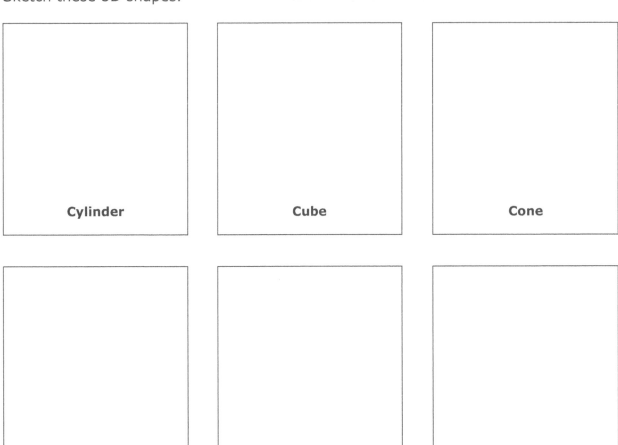

Cylinder

Cube

Cone

Cuboid

Triangular prism

Sphere

2 Complete these two drawings of a cube and a cuboid.

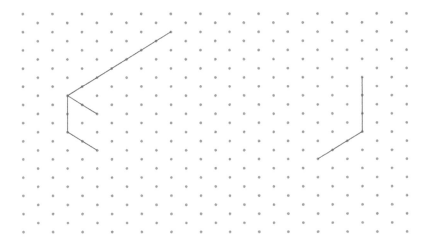

MyMaths.co.uk

Q 1078   SEARCH

Here are 2 isometric drawings.
For each drawing, draw a **plan view**, a **front elevation** and a **side elevation**.

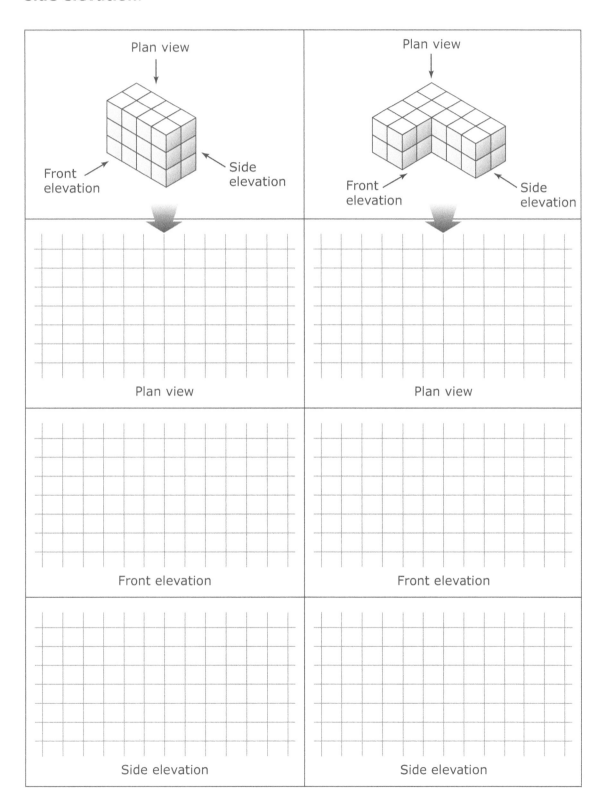

Plan view

Front elevation   Side elevation

Plan view   Plan view

Front elevation   Front elevation

Side elevation   Side elevation

Plan view

Front elevation   Side elevation

I can do
this page!

1 These solid shapes are made from 1 cm cubes.

What is the volume of each shape?

a

_____ cm³

b

_____ cm³

c
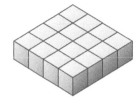

_____ cm³

d
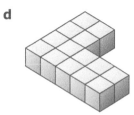

_____ cm³

2 This cuboid has a volume of 9 cm³.

a A second layer of cubes is added.
What is the new volume?

_____ cm³

b A third layer of cubes is added.
What is the new volume?

_____ cm³

3 What are the volumes of these cuboids?

a

_____ cm³

b

_____ cm³

c

_____ cm³

MyMaths.co.uk

Q 1137   SEARCH

1   These cuboids are made from **centimetre cubes**.

   What is the volume of each cuboid?

a

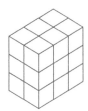

Volume = _____ cm³

b

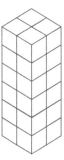

Volume = _____ cm³

c

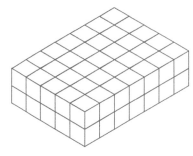

Volume = _____ cm³

2   Use the formula   Volume = length × width × height

   to find the volume of these cuboids.

a

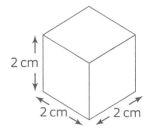

2 cm

2 cm   2 cm

Volume = _____ cm³

b

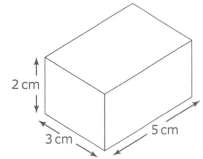

2 cm

3 cm   5 cm

Volume = _____ cm³

c

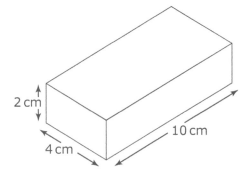

2 cm

4 cm   10 cm

Volume = _____ cm³

d

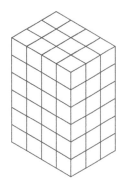

Volume = _____ cm³

1   Sketch the net of this cuboid and calculate its surface area.

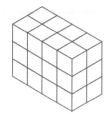

> The surface area is the total area of all the faces.

Surface area = _____ cm²

2   This drawing of a cuboid shows the **plan view**, the **side elevation** and the **front elevation**.

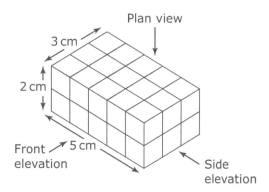

a   What is the area of the plan view?   _____ cm²

b   What is the area of the side elevation?   _____ cm²

c   What is the area of the front elevation?   _____ cm²

d   The cuboid has 6 faces; what is the total surface area of the cuboid?   _____ cm²

Case study 5: The golden rectangle

The golden rectangle has fascinated scholars for over 2000 years. It's a special kind of rectangle, which is often found in art and architecture.

Task 1

Rectangles come in all shapes and sizes, or different **proportions**. Here are six different rectangles. They can be sorted into three pairs of **similar** rectangles.

3 cm

15 cm

4 cm

1 cm [A]   5 cm [B]   9 cm [C]

6 cm

2 cm

8 cm

4 cm [D]   3 cm [E]   2 cm [F]

a Write down which pairs of rectangles are similar.
b For each rectangle, divide the longer side by the shorter side and write down the result.
   i What do you notice?
   ii What can you say about similar rectangles and the **ratio** of their sides?

$$A:B = B:C$$
or
$$\frac{A}{B} = \frac{B}{C}$$

Task 2

Here is a square with a smaller square next to it.
Together they form a larger rectangle.

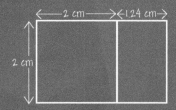

2 cm — 1.24 cm

2 cm

a Look at the larger rectangle.
   Divide the longer side by the shorter side and write down the result, to 1 d.p.
b Now look at the smaller rectangle and do the same. What do you notice? Describe your findings using the word 'similar' if possible.

Did you Know
One possible place where the golden ratio occurs is in the ratio of your height to the top of your head, to the height to your navel.

15a Ratio

1 In this pattern the ratio of white to blue counters is 2 : 1

   Add counters to these patterns so that the ratio is the same.

a 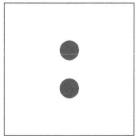   b 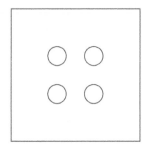   c

2 In this pattern the ratio of blue triangles to white triangles is 1 : 4

   Add blue triangles to these patterns so that the ratio is the same.

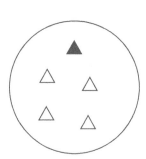

a 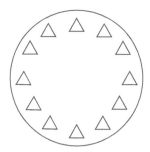   b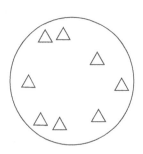

3 These patterns should all have the same ratio of blue tiles to white tiles.

   Some tiles are missing from **a** and **b**.

   Complete the patterns.

Correct ratio 1 : 3

a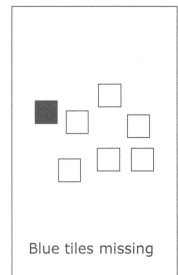

Blue tiles missing

b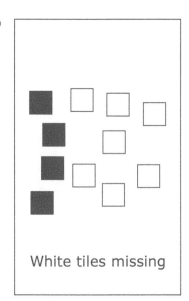

White tiles missing

MyMaths.co.uk   Q 1052   SEARCH

15b Dividing in a given ratio

1   a   Here are 16 coins. Share them into 2 piles in the ratio 3:1.

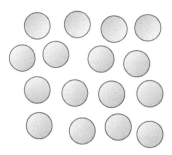

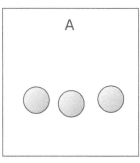

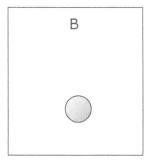

   b   Write the number of coins in each pile.

   Pile A: _____ coins

   Pile B: _____ coins

2   a   Divide 18 coins into 2 piles in the ratio 1:5.

   Use this space for your drawing.

   b   How many coins are there in each pile?   Pile A: _____ coins   Pile B: _____ coins

3   Divide £30 in the ratio 2:3. The answer has been started for you.

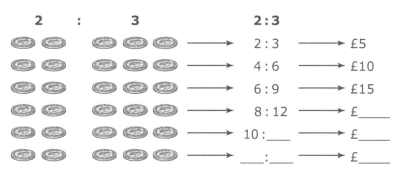

2	:	3		2:3		

2:3 ⟶ £5
4:6 ⟶ £10
6:9 ⟶ £15
8:12 ⟶ £_____
10:___ ⟶ £_____
___:___ ⟶ £_____

£30 shared in the ratio 2:3 is £ _____ and £ _____.

4   Divide £24 in the ratio 5:1.

   Use this space for your drawing.

   £24 shared in the ratio 5:1 is £ _____ : £ _____.

1   Here is a recipe for bread and butter pudding.

It makes enough for 4 people.

a   Complete this table.

Some parts have been done to help you.

> 8 slices of bread
> 2 eggs
> 200 ml milk
> 50 g sugar
> 250 g sultanas

	bread (slices)	eggs	milk (ml)	sugar (g)	sultanas (g)
2 people					125
8 people	16	4			

b   Complete this table for the recipe for 10 people.

	bread (slices)	eggs	milk (ml)	sugar (g)	sultanas (g)
10 people					

2   Concrete is made from cement, sand, gravel and water.

This mixture makes enough concrete for one eighth $\left(\frac{1}{8}\right)$ of a shed floor.

> Cement   30 kg
> Sand   90 kg
> Gravel   20 kg
> Water   7 litres

Complete the table to work out the mixture to concrete the whole floor.

	cement (kg)	sand (kg)	gravel (kg)	water (litres)
$\frac{1}{8}$ of the floor	30	90		
whole floor				

1 Josh wants to buy 6 chocolate biscuits.
   A multi-pack of 6 biscuits costs £1.44.
   Single biscuits cost 27p each.

   How much will Josh save if he buys the multi-pack?

£1.44

CHOC 27p

Money saved = _____ p

2 TJ has 6 small coins in his pocket.
   He knows that 3 of them are 5p coins and 2 are 1p coins.

   He also knows that the probability of taking a 5p coin from his pocket is $\frac{1}{2}$.

   Is the unknown coin a 5p or a 1p?   1p ☐   5p ☐

3 A litre of petrol cost £1.35 in 2014.
   In 1989 a litre cost 15p.
   How many litres of petrol could have been bought for 90p in 1989?

   _____ litres

4 Jamie has £5 to spend at the school fete.
   He has 3 tries at 'Beat the Goalie' at 50p a go.
   He then buys 2 ice creams for 75p each.
   How much money has he got left?

   Money left = £_____

5 A glass holds 300 ml.
   How many glasses can Hari fill from a 2 litre bottle of cola?

   _____ glasses

6 A recipe needs 3 eggs to make 36 cookies.

   a Amani has only 1 egg. How many cookies can she make?

   _____ cookies

   b How many cookies could she make with 2 eggs?

   _____ cookies

1   These four bags contain blue and white beads.

From each outcome below, draw an arrow to the probability line to estimate
the probability of each event.

The probability of picking a blue bead from bag A	The probability of picking a blue bead from bag D	The probability of picking a white bead from bag C	The probability of picking a white bead from bag B

Impossible   Even chance   Certain

2   You have 2 blue beads and 2 white beads.

Draw your beads in these empty bags so that the probability statements are true.
You do not need to use all the beads each time.

a   The probability of picking a blue
bead is 1.

b   There is an even chance of picking
a white bead or a blue bead.

c   The probability of picking a blue
bead is more than an even chance,
but less than certain.

d   It is impossible to pick a white bead.

MyMaths.co.uk   Q 1209   SEARCH

1 Here are some blue and white cubes in bags.

   A   B   C   D

a Which bag would give you a $\frac{1}{4}$ chance of picking a blue cube? _____

b Which bag would give you a $\frac{1}{5}$ chance of picking a white cube? _____

c Which bag would give you no chance of picking a blue cube? _____

d Which bag would give you a $\frac{2}{5}$ chance of picking a white cube? _____

e Which bag would give you a certain chance of picking a white cube? _____

2 Tick the statement that best describes the probable outcome in each event.

a This spinner is fair.

   i The probability of Danny winning is $\frac{1}{2}$ ☐

   ii The probability of Danny winning is $\frac{1}{10}$ ☐

   iii The probability of Danny winning is $\frac{1}{5}$ ☐

b This dice is fair.

   i The probability of Lorna getting 6 is $\frac{3}{4}$ ☐

   ii The probability of Lorna getting 6 is $\frac{3}{5}$ ☐

   iii The probability of Lorna getting 6 is $\frac{1}{6}$ ☐

c Here are 10 cards – one of them is an ace.

   i The chances of Kelvin picking an ace at random is $\frac{3}{10}$ ☐

   ii The chances of Kelvin picking an ace at random is $\frac{1}{10}$ ☐

   iii The chances of Kelvin picking an ace at random is $\frac{1}{5}$ ☐

1 This probability scale is marked in percentages and fractions.

| 0% | 10% | 20% | 30% | 40% | 50% | 60% | 70% | 80% | 90% | 100% |

0 $\frac{1}{10}$ $\frac{2}{10}$ $\frac{3}{10}$ $\frac{4}{10}$ $\frac{5}{10}$ $\frac{6}{10}$ $\frac{7}{10}$ $\frac{8}{10}$ $\frac{9}{10}$ 1

Use the probability scale to convert:

a $\frac{1}{10}$ = _____ % **b** 80% = _____ **c** 50% = _____ **d** $\frac{9}{10}$ = _____ %

2 Complete this probability scale by writing the percentages.

_____%   _____%   _____%   _____%   _____%

0 $\frac{1}{4}$ $\frac{2}{4}=\frac{1}{2}$ $\frac{3}{4}$ $\frac{4}{4}=1$

3 Draw 10 beads in each bag to show the given percentage probabilities.

The first one is done for you.

a probability of
blue = 40%

b probability of
white = 70%

c probability of
blue = 10%

d probability of
white = 100%

e probability of
blue = 50%

f probability of
blue = 70%

MyMaths.co.uk

Q 1210   SEARCH

1 Mel and Jack have 3 cards each.

They take turns to put down 1 card at random.
They add the 2 values together to give their score.

The table shows all of the possible added scores.

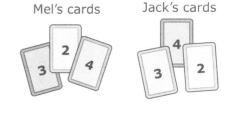

Mel's cards   Jack's cards

Mel's cards

+	**2**	**3**	**4**
2	4		
3	5		7
4			

Jack's cards

a Complete the table by **adding** the numbers on their pairs of cards.

b How many different outcomes are there altogether? _____

c What is the probability of scoring an even number? _____

d What is the probability of scoring an odd number? _____

2 Mel and Jack play the game again.

Mel's cards   Jack's cards

This time they **multiply** the numbers on their cards to give their scores.

Mel's cards

×	**2**	**3**	**4**
2			
3			
4			

Jack's cards

a Complete the table.

b What is the probability that their multiplied score will be more than 10? _____

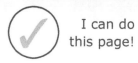
1   Write these probabilities in their simplest form.
    The first one is done for you.

    a $\div 2$ $\dfrac{6}{8} = \dfrac{3}{4}$ $\div 2$

    b $\dfrac{5}{10} =$ ____

    c $\dfrac{9}{12} =$ ____

    d $\dfrac{6}{9} =$ ____

    e $\dfrac{2}{10} =$ ____

    > Hint: Look for a number that will divide into the numerator and the denominator.

2   Write the probability of picking a white bead at random as
    a fraction and as a percentage.

    a

    b

    c

    d

    ____ or ____ %   ____ or ____ %   ____ or ____ %   ____ or ____ %

3   The probability of picking a white bead at random from this set is 25%

    (1 chance in 4 or $\dfrac{1}{4}$).

    a Shade these beads so that the
           probability of picking a white
           bead is 25%.

    b Shade these beads so that
           the probability of picking a
           white bead is 75%.

    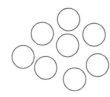

4   Shade each set of tiles so that the probability of picking a shaded tile is 20%.

    10 tiles   20 tiles   5 tiles

    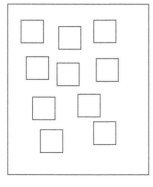      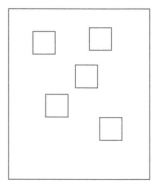

MyMaths.co.uk   🔍 1211   SEARCH

Forensic experts have used mathematical techniques to solve crimes for a long time. Probability, formulae and graphs are three of the topics that they need to be familiar with.

The Weekly Bugle

Following a jewellery shop raid in Park Street, Tooting, on Saturday afternoon, a getway car was found abandoned at the junction with Fisher Row. The Ford Fiesta had narrowly missed a cyclist after skidding 60 metres. Police investigaing the incident are keen to trace the driver of the car.

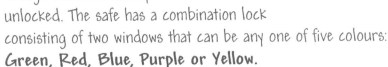

Task 1

Detectives searching for clues at the jewellery shop notice that a safe has been tampered with, though not successfully unlocked. The safe has a combination lock consisting of two windows that can be any one of five colours: **Green, Red, Blue, Purple or Yellow.**

Only one combination will open the safe. How many possible combinations are there?

TYRE MARKS   CONFIDENTIAL

Task 2

The length of the tyre marks left by a skidding car depends on its speed when it started skidding.

Initial speed	length of tyre marks
20 mph	5 metres
40 mph	20 metres
60 mph	45 metres
80 mph	80 metres

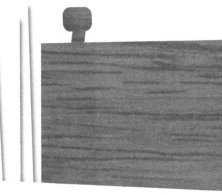

a   Use the data to complete the graph of the length of the tyre marks against speed.
b   Join the points with a smooth line.
c   Extend your graph to get an approximate speed for the car in the news article. (60 metres)

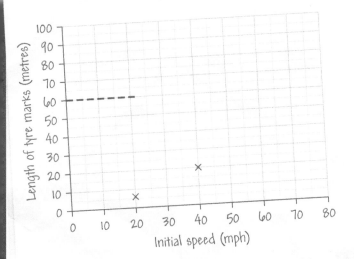

This fence is constructed from **panels** and held in place with **supports**.

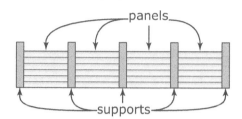

Each panel costs £3.00
Each support costs £2.00

1   What is the cost of each fence?

a

£ _____

b

£ _____

c

£ _____

d

£ _____

2   Fence **d** is twice as long as fence **c**. Does fence **d** cost twice as much as fence **c**?

Show your working.

Fence **c** costs £ _____   Fence **d** costs £ _____

3   You have £50.00. Draw the longest complete fence you can make with this amount of money.

I can do
this page!

These different lengths of fence are made from **panels** and **supports**.

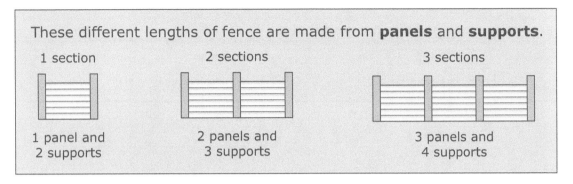

1 section	2 sections	3 sections
1 panel and 2 supports	2 panels and 3 supports	3 panels and 4 supports

This information has been recorded onto this table.

Number of panels	1	2	3							
Number of supports	2	3	4							

1   Continue to fill in this table up to the tenth panel.

2   What pattern can you see that links the number of panels to the number of supports?

_____

_____

These fences are made from **posts** and **chains**.

1 section	2 sections	3 sections	4 sections
2 posts and 2 chains	3 posts and 4 chains	4 posts and 6 chains	5 posts and 8 chains

This information has been recorded onto this table.

Number of posts	2	3	4	5						
Number of chains	2	4	6	8						

3   Continue to fill in this table up to the tenth section.

4   What pattern can you see that links **posts** and **chains**?

_____

_____

 I can do this page!

These fences are made from **panels** and **supports**.

1 section

1 panel and
2 supports

2 sections

2 panels and
3 supports

3 sections

3 panels and
4 supports

1 Tick the statement that describes the link between **panels** and **supports**.

   a For each panel there are 2 supports.

   b The number of supports is always 1 more than the number of panels.

   c The number of panels is always 1 more than the number of supports.

2 Tick the rule that describes the link between panels and supports.
   (*p* stands for panels. *s* stands for supports.)

   $p - 1 = s$

   $p = 2s$

   $p + 1 = s$

These fences are made from **posts** and **chains**.

1 section

2 chains and
2 posts

2 sections

4 chains and
3 posts

3 sections

6 chains and
4 posts

4 sections

8 chains and
5 posts

3 Tick the statement that describes the link between **posts** and **chains**.

   a The number of posts, times 2, equals the number of chains.

   b The number of posts, add 2, equals the number of chains.

   c The number of posts, times 2, then subtract 2, equals the number of chains.

4 Tick the rule that describes the link between posts and chains.
   (*p* stands for posts. *c* stands for chains.)

   $2p = c$

   $2p - 2 = c$

   $p + 1 = c$

MyMaths.co.uk

This fence is made from **panels** and **supports**.

Each panel costs **£3.00** and each support costs **£2.00**.

The costs are written in this table:

Number of panels	1	2	3	4	5	6	7	8	9	10
Cost (£)	7	12	17	22	27	32	37	42	47	52

1 a Plot this data onto the graph. The first 2 points have been done for you.

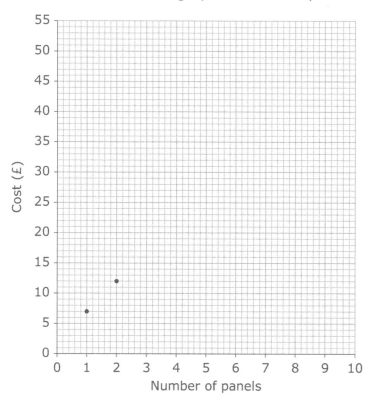

The rule that links the number of **panels** and the **cost** is: **2 + 5n = cost**
where **n** is the number of panels.
To find the cost of 10 panels: **2 + 5 × 10 = 52**

b Use the rule to calculate the cost of a fence 20 panels long.   £_____

c Use the rule to calculate the cost of a fence 25 panels long.   £_____

d Use the rule to calculate the cost of a fence 100 panels long.   £_____

Checklist – I can do it!

Multiplication table

×	1	2	3	4	5	6	7	8	9	10	11	12
1	1	2	3	4	5	6	7	8	9	10	11	12
2	2	4	6	8	10	12	14	16	18	20	22	24
3	3	6	9	12	15	18	21	24	27	30	33	36
4	4	8	12	16	20	24	28	32	36	40	44	48
5	5	10	15	20	25	30	35	40	45	50	55	60
6	6	12	18	24	30	36	42	48	54	60	66	72
7	7	14	21	28	35	42	49	56	63	70	77	84
8	8	16	24	32	40	48	56	64	72	80	88	96
9	9	18	27	36	45	54	63	72	81	90	99	108
10	10	20	30	40	50	60	70	80	90	100	110	120
11	11	22	33	44	55	66	77	88	99	110	121	132
12	12	24	36	48	60	72	84	96	108	120	132	144